50 Rules of Politics

CHARLES MWEWA

Republished by:

AFRICA IN CANADA PRESS
Ottawa, Ontario
Canada
acpress.ca
charlesmwewa.com

ISBN: 9781703467710

DEDICATION

For

Martin Bwalya Mulenga

CONTENTS

AUTHOR'S WORDS

I love politics. I love law. I love religion. There is nothing in the world that we do without involving any one of these three. They affect us whether we know it or not, or whether we like it or not. The systems of the nations are governed by these three instruments.

This little book is a Rule-Guide on politics. It is meant to be an on-the-spot-guide. Politicians all over the world will find it handy and ready to use. It is written in notation format, of concise, terse but easy-to-understand hints and points. It covers all of the politics' life – from strategy to tactics, to campaigning to rallying the voters, to voting, and to governance.

No-one is born a politician. There is no special natural-born trait that makes a politician. Politics is observation. Politics may be learned by participating in politics. Politics may be borne from exercising one's civic liberties and responsibilities. Political skills may also be acquired by studying the lives of great political minds and politicians. No-one means of acquiring political ability is superior to another.

What is, however, common to all politics and politicians, is the desire and the dedication to improve the lives of the people. In that regard, therefore, politics is the instrument of distributing national resources and the management of human affairs within a nation. It is born out of trust and grows into responsibility.

Anyone can be a politician – if they desire to lead their people with equity, justice and righteousness. Most politics is competitive. To ace the political arena, these rules are essential.

c.m.

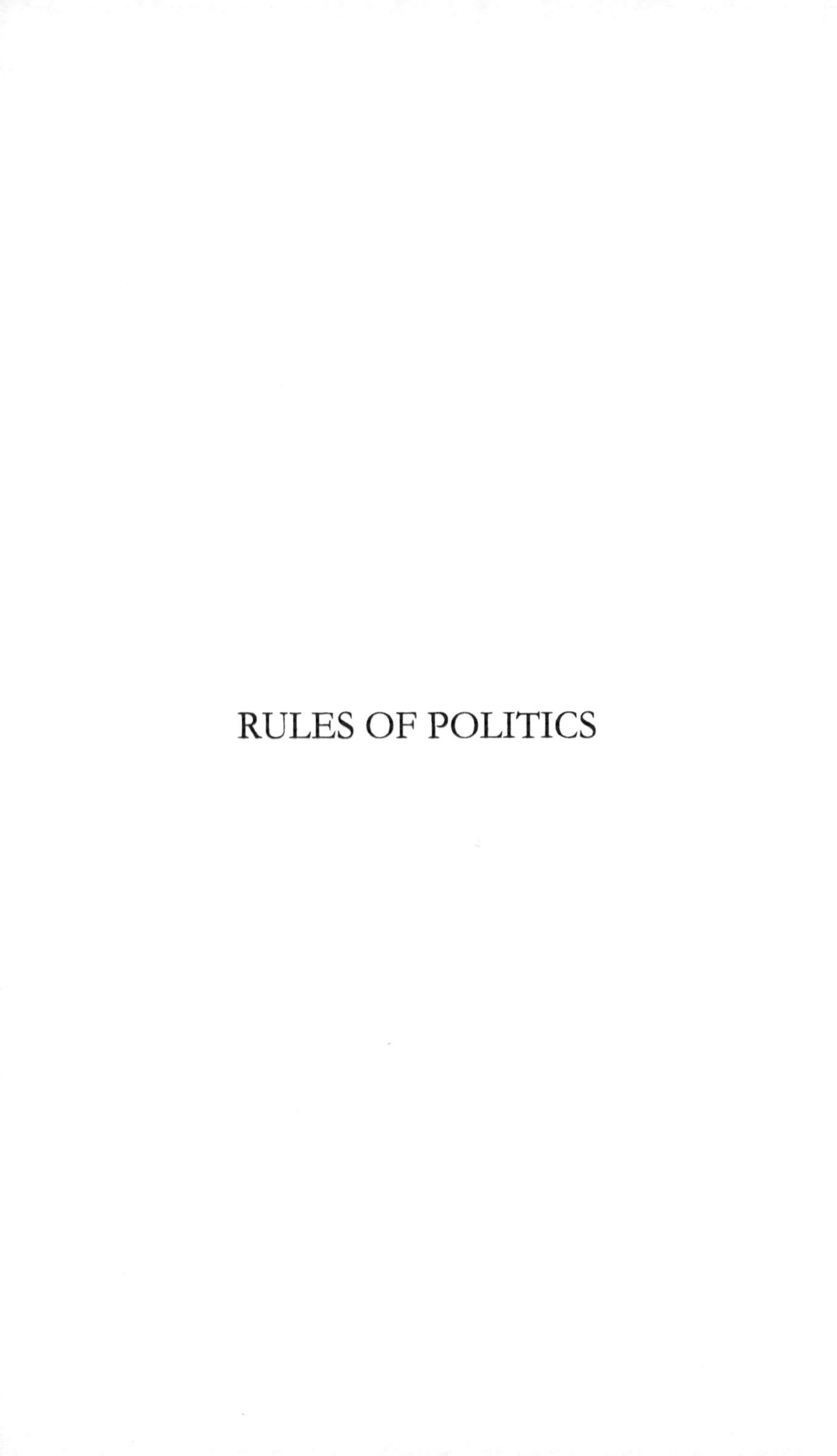

RULES OF POLITICS

RULE #1. PERCEPTION IS CURRENCY

– things can be or they cannot be, but let people perceive them to be favorable to you, and to them. Your win must always be a loss for a competitor. In politics, how people see you is more important than who you actually are. Politics is not religion, and perception is currency.

RULE #2. GUARD THE BRAND

– people relate politics to a name or names, guard the brand jealously. If your strength/brand is the candidate, rally every troop to shelter his or her territory and character. In democratic politics, a good name is equal to longevity. A bad name will shortly be defeated by a good one – just introduce another brand and the old brand will be forgotten.

RULE #3. PEOPLE OVER PLAN

– it may seem a contradiction with reality, but in politics, people want to be seen to come first. They want to *feel* they come first. They want to *hear* they come first. They *love* to hear they come first, even if deep down their hearts they may know that you are not being candid with them.

RULE #4. LEADER'S WEAKNESSES ARE STRENGTHS

– you never accept or seem to concede that your leader has weaknesses. To the electorate, a leader is almost infallible (and even when they know he or she is human), they just want to hear that he or she is always right, always strong and always there. If the leader has weaknesses, they want to hear that, in fact, those are strengths by another name. They may turn an apology into blame ownership.

RULE #5. ALWAYS COMPARE WITH AN OPPOSITION

– don't compare the politician to another politician only if that politician is an opponent in an election. In other words, let the voters feel that you are exactly like everyone else except your competitor. That way, when the people enter the booth, they only see you and your opponent and immediately rule your opponent out. It's that simple.

RULE #6. MAKE AN OPPONENT'S ONE WEAKNESS ALL THEIR WEAKNESSES

– thus, if they can do this, they can do that and that and that. But make your one strength your all strengths – thus, because you can do this or you are this, then you are all these other good things or you can do all these other good things.

RULE #7. YOUR RIDING IS YOUR LANDING

– are you vying for a national stage, a constituency or a municipal portfolio, it does not matter. Make that stage your fall to place. "I am doing this because of [my country, area, constituency, and etc.]" In other words, you are nothing without your riding – if you fail to win the election, your riding should suffer from what could have been had you won. Of course, you will win. Your riding comes first, not your family or your personal interests (if that's also your agenda, then do not disclose.)

RULE #8. SPEAK THE PEOPLE'S LANGUAGE

– that is, speak the people's language, relate to them, feel and sound like them. If possible, quote the local poets and remind them of their own great people. Culture is deeply imbued in language expressions, and these people are already familiar with their own heroes. All you are trying to be is their next hero. Tailor your message to demography – age, population density, social classification, educational attainments, historical disparities, and so on. People, intuitively, relate to a candidate who recognizes their constituencies and subliminally supports them.

RULE #9. PAINT A PICTURE

– people remember most what is graphic and leaves a picture in their minds. Demonstrate before them. Sketch their problems and the proposed solutions. Let the people "see" how you will be different from anyone else, the opponent. This entails the power of persuasion. Do not leave things to chances or to commonly acceptable standards. If it is during the Covid-19 pandemic, for example, highlight the people's fears but at the same time offer them hope. Persuade them through words or otherwise, to believe that, with you, things will turn out just fine. People are looking for a "savior" in crisis times and a listener in good times.

RULE #10. SHOWCASE 90% WHAT – 10% HOW MATRIX

– people want to fall in love with a person and what he or she is promising before they hear how he or she will reach there (this, too, is contrary to what is assumed to be logical.) It's wise to devote 90% of your campaign or time to telling the people "What" you will do and achieve for them. Just towards the election day, then reveal your platform – the "How" you will reach there. This leaves the brilliant analyst with little time to scrutinize your platform, and since the people have already internalized *you*, they will vote for you, anyway.

RULE #11. INVOKE THE PEOPLE TO VOTE, ANY CHANCE YOU GET

– people feel "sent" when they reach the ballot booth/box. The politician who challenged people to go out and vote will usually receive more votes. Why? Because people behave as if he or she has "sent" them there, to vote.

RULE #12. PREPARATION IS KEY

– don't appear in public without preparation. Don't go to speak to the media without a signature attire, smile or characteristic. Don't be caught unaware – your unkempt last-appearance could be the only thing people remember. Even if you didn't prepare well, remember Rule #1, create the perception that you are prepared. If people feel that you are working hard for them, they will think that you will work hard for them.

RULE #13. DON'T MIX UP NUMBERS/FACTS

– get your figures and facts right. Do your calculations right. Review history, if possible, unless you can spin it to look like, "I was just joking." Prepare well and rehearse before debates, before delivering a key-note speech and, generally, when you are called upon to represent your party or nation.

RULE #14. STUDY YOUR OPPONENT

– you cannot assume your opponent will say this or that or do this or that, *anticipate* they will. Study their mannerisms and understand both their strengths and weaknesses and tailor these or compare them to your own. You fall only because you don't know, not because you *did* know.

RULE #15. ALWAYS HAVE YOUR OWN VERSION OF THE STORY

– a strategic politician wants to whirl their own version of things. People fail to write-down a candidate on two sets of stories on the issue. They seem to want to know which is the better or correct version, but in party politics, the time factor is gold. You only accept the opponent's version of the story if it helps you. Otherwise, it is political suicide to accept what your opponent says without a reasonable rebuttal.

RULE #16. TRUTH IS RELATIVE

– politics is not religion; it is an exercise in civic responsibility. Since it caters to a larger array of ideas and viewpoints, truth is transacted in relativity rather than in absolutes. Idea synthesis is key. A true politician looks at all views and embraces and becomes all things to all people. He may not be a scientist, but he or she must embrace some saliences of science; they may not be Muslims, but they must embrace some saliences of Islam; and they may not belong to a particular race, tribe or caste, but they must embrace saliences of all these aggregates. Legacy is only possible where a politician considers all the people as important – the young, old, women, men and so on.

RULE #17. PROMISE PERMISSIVENESS

– good politicians do not use promises as means to an end; promises are the ends. Politics is deeply rooted in making good, wide and believable promises. The fulfillment of promises is not the ultimate goal of democratic politicking – promises are tied to the Rule of Law. Hence, being agenda-driven, a good politician will strive to translate some or all of their promises into legislation but this must not be taken as the ultimate goal. Compulsory process requires only that promises were made and efforts were made to attempt to translate them into law. A politician should not be indicted on the premise that their promises never became law; success should be measured on the efforts made. This is so because of Rule #18.

RULE #18. PRIORITIES MAY SUPERSEDE PROMISES

– in parliamentary democracy, the party with the majority Members of Parliament (MPs) forms government. In presidential democracy, the person who wins the presidency, their party also wins a tenure in power. Once the mandate is given by an election, the politician must choose wisely among various competing demands and prioritize the management of promises. Democratic politics is tenure-based, it may not be feasible to implement all promises or to translate all of them into law in a limited space of time. Setting reachable, attainable and pragmatic priorities is vital to keeping the electorates happy. And good politics thrives on constant communication with the electorate, the people, on why certain promises were delayed or would have to wait.

RULE #19. ASSUMPTION IS LIABILITY

– political geniuses know that to assume what people want is an error. To know what the people need, is golden. A politician must invest in research and analysis. There are no two ways about it. A smart politician must sense the "mood" in which people are and integrate their views and strategies into it. A politician can either create a mood or tap into the one already existing. The secret is to always *be one with the people*.

RULE #20. TELL THE PEOPLE WHAT THEY WANT TO HEAR

– politics is not preaching. It is not lecturing, either. You don't tell people what you want them to know. People want you to tell them what they want to hear or what they want to know. Tell the people to vote for you whether they love or hate you – because "I love you all, regardless. And your problems are my problems, and your hardships are mine, too." If there is a constituency that supports your views, preach to the choir. If the constituency you face does not endorse your views, listen to them, and offer a willingness to adapt to their needs.

RULE #21. RESTATE SUCCESSES, EXPLAIN FAILURES

– this should be an all-season mantra. People forget. Remind them often of all the successes you are making or have made. When you fail to fulfill a promise or you encounter legislation failure, immediately explain to the people. Keep doing this for as long as you remain a politician: *Restate your successes and explain your failures.*

RULE #22. SPIN IS NOT A SIN

– a good politician must be a master of spin. This is anchored in Rule #16. Politics is not a judicial theater, and truth is relative. Always find a way to explain a point, an event, a view or a development. Spin is not a sin; it's how you view things. There is a thin line between not being credible and a sheer skill at embellishing your own reality of things. Life is not linear; and people experience life differently. The job of a good politician is to justify their spins.

RULE #23. ALWAYS ANSWER A QUESTION EVEN IF YOU DON'T ANSWER IT

– in other words, always say something or provide some explanation to an inquiry. Silence when silence is not required, is political liability. At first instance, this tactic may look like dodging or even immoral, but reality dictates otherwise. If you fail to answer a question or provide an explanation, you lose in general credibility to the electorate.

RULE #24. CHARISMA IS CATALYST

– keep things interesting. Charm the people. Dazzle their minds. Create excitement. This is how this ancient syllogism works: *People love to listen and believe someone who seem to know and believe in what they are transacting.* If you display charisma for the proposition you are selling to the electorate, they will, therefore, be interested in it and will support you. This has never failed to awaken disinterested folks who end up lifting you up to glory. If you are slow, dull and unassuming, people may not take you seriously. Keep this excitement to the election day; people may change their minds a minute before they vote.

RULE #25. FASHION IS BASTION

– be a statement, exult style and embrace a peculiar fashion. Your style is your fortress – it will protect you. If you have no sense of style or fashion, people will compare you to the ideal and the obvious, and you may fall short. From the onset of politicking, set a peculiar fashion tone and stick to it. If you wear a mustache, stick to it. If you prefer going bored, keep it that way. That will be your statement and it will form your stronghold. This, too, simplifies you for your audience and makes them feel comfortable with you. It is not simply what you can do; *it is what you must do.*

RULE #26. MILD POLITICAL CORRECTNESS

– use political correctness, mildly, and only to win over your opponent, thereafter rule and be politically incorrect.

RULE #27. ALWAYS A LEARNER

– in politics, you are always a student: Study what makes people cynical and disillusioned, and fix them.

RULE #28. MAKE NEW NEWS

– do not allow your opponent to move first, to break new news before you. Always engineer ways in which you are the news breaker. That way, you will always have the media credit you, directly or indirectly. In politics, *be the news*, daily.

RULE #29. ANTI-TRIBAL WIZARDRY

– get sick when you talk about tribalism, racialism or *castism*. People want to know you care about such issues. Don't simply read a statement. State in no uncertain terms: "I am not a tribalist; I am not a racist."

RULE #30. CHANGE IS BOTTOM-UP

– somehow everyone thinks that the politicians make change happen, that's a fallacy. Real change is prompted and maintained by the people. When people organize and demand change, political leadership should answer. Grassroots campaign, similarly, is the best and easiest way to galvanize the masses for political change. Feed the people with good reasons why they should demand change, and they will bring change. A clever politician reads the tides and rides on them, with the masses.

RULE #31. SURVIVAL IS REVIVAL

– politics is, anatomically, a bone of endurance. Each day, there will be mud thrown at you. You should not allow any to stick on you – though you can't avoid it thrown at you. Don't be re-branded.

RULE #32. SCANDALS HAVE LIFESPAN

– the nature of scandals is that they have a birth date, a life and they die. If a scandal cannot be killed in infancy, it must be neutralized as it grows, evidently making it harmless. Time is the best umpire. The longer a scandal persists, the easier it is to spin it into a distraction. A scandal is only effective the shortest lifespan it has. Thus, if you have something to bring against your opponent, wait a few days before the elections. Because, then it will be fresh as the people vote. If one is leveled against you close to election time, do not keep silent, say something to diminish its potency, as well as propagandizing to the electorate what you believe is or are the real problems they face. You may accept the scandal is real or did happen, but then transfer the blame to someone or something else. As people try to figure out the other blameworthy individual or thing, elections would have taken place and you would have received your vote.

RULE #33. OPPORTUNISM IS RESOURCEFULNESS

– elsewhere you will be accused of being an opportunist, but not in politics. If you cannot take down a wounded buffalo, you are in dangerous territories when it recovers. If you cannot knock down a wimpy, dazed and unstable boxer, you are in deep trouble when she stabilizes. Do your job while your opponent stumbles. As they say, "Finish him." Elsewhere, that could be wrong, and even immoral, but not in politics.

RULE #34. LAW OF SUSTENANCE

– you can call it whatever you want, if you cannot sustain a story that hurts the political interests of the other side, you have not mastered the skills necessary for political manumission. Keep hitting hard on the opponent with what is working. If the rates are going up, your favorability is skyrocketing or you keep winning by a certain story, keep it going. Sustain it until it is no longer effective. Keep repeating the same line over and over. Monotony only finds it's heroism in politics. It is the same reason why slogans, mottoes, jingles, chants and repeated campaign songs work in politics.

RULE #35. MASTER IN MODERATE MUDSLING

— mudslinging is the art of making malicious or scandalous allegations about an opponent with the aim of damaging their reputation. Depending on which side you find yourself, either have a damage control strategy (see Rule #7) or have some moderate mud slides. You will be wise to use them in moderation. If people think that you are only looking for malicious ways to discredit your opponent, it could backfire on you.

RULE #36. ISSUES THAT MATTER

– even in overtly uncivilized worlds, in any political cycle, there are issues that matter to people. It could be the economy (bread and butter issues), foreign policy, poverty, and etc., and a good politician remembers to address these issues. People relate well to a candidate who seems to focus and speak to what they are confronting on the day-to-day basis.

RULE #37. NEVER PREACH VIOLENCE

– don't even imply it in your campaigning or statements. Preaching violence has a boomerang effect and can cause serious jeopardy to democracy and its principles of tolerance and smart government. A politician who ignores their violent caders or riles them up into violence is doing a disservice to politics in general. Where there has been violence, a politician should condemn such in the strongest terms.

RULE #38. EMOTIONAL CONTROL

– in politics, you get to be asked the same questions over and over again. Usually, in general living, such repetitious questioning can be a source of anger and frustration. But never in politics. You must always repeat your answer even if it has been asked 1000 times. Never show any anger or frustration, simply answer, graciously and competently as if you are hearing the question for the very first time. Refer to Rule #39 for further clarification.

RULE #39. RULE OF FORTY-NINE INSANITY

– in politics, you must be insane at least 49 percent of the time. The *Rule of Insanity* is normalcy in politics because each time you meet people, they have no idea who you had met before. So, people are expected to probe you on the same issue others did.

Your thinking should not be retrospective but prospective, as if you are encountering the people and their questions for the first time. Normalcy will return after elections. Before that, let your mind wander just as issues may be emerging from everywhere. But bearing in mind Rule #39, keep your emotions under control and dance to the people's tune, if necessary.

RULE #40. DEFENDING THE INDEFENSIBLE

– unless you can't do so without miring yourself in deep trouble, avoid defending what is clear and plain before the people.

RULE #41. MINIMUM INFORMATION, MAXIMUM REFORMATION

– a politician is not a journalist, sometimes the two roles could be so close that they may be mistaken or could overlap. It is the duty of journalists to inform, not of politicians. Political rhetoric should concentrate on policy and implementation. The duo ideals of policy and implementation favor *reformation* rather than *information*. Unless in informing a politician is advancing a position least understood or is providing evidence to prove or disprove a claim, majority of the time should be spent on reforms. Thus, a politician should make announcements, statements and clarifications. When elected, this should continue as legislation (enacted law) or policy implementation tools.

RULE #42. MEDIA LOVE-TRAP

– however hard they may try; the media is a human institution and emotions and favoritism reign supreme. Therefore, accept media love cautiously. The rule is not to over-engage to the extent that you trust the media wholly to transmit your views. As long as media remains for profit, it will always love you for as long as you have not gaffed. When it is not in its interest, the media may dump you just as fast. Your perfection or imperfections may not matter much to the media, but your profitability does. To the media, news may be more important than views. However, in modern society, politics and a free media shall always coexist.

RULE #43. PANDER BLUNDER

— many a politician believes that their views will be communicated correctly by the media. That is thinking best tempered with caveat. The media like to report your politics from its own perspectives. Do not buy too much in what the pundits gloat over. If one member of the media says something bad about you or your policies, do not vow revenge; it's just the nature of politics-media relationship when it comes to politicking. Rather, presume your views will be misreported until they are not. Give the media a benefit of the doubt. The reason is simple: If you lean towards a certain view and a media house adheres towards the same, your views are likely to be reported not only accurately but with an exaggerated pastiche, but in your favor. The opposite is the case if the media house does not prefer your view. In the latter case, remain composed, and make written statements and press releases.

RULE #44. WHEN YOUR OPPONENT SAYS YOU'RE WRONG

– you may be right. Politics is a *single-glory street*, it rarely stops at the "You are right boulevard." That means that if you craft a plan, policy or agenda and your opponents say it is wrong, without giving any alternatives, chances are you're right. Do not fall into the trap of second-guessing your agenda, simply show the electorate that your opponent lacks an alternative plan or what they have advanced is shaky or unattainable. If your opponent brings out an alternative agenda, it is incumbent upon you to making comparable submissions and ask the voters to prefer your plan. Remember Rule #11.

RULE #45. IF YOUR OPPONENT SAYS YOU'RE RIGHT

– it means you are right. But only if your opponent doesn't proffer an advanced or a superior simulant. If your opponent merely praises your project, plan, agenda or policy, and does not give a superior alternative, take advantage of the praise and communicate, in your opponent's own words, to the voters or the people. It is also preferable to create TV ads and place your opponent in the center of advancing your agenda. If your opponent agrees with you or your policy and does, indeed, provide a simulant, you have to react as in Rule #44.

RULE #46. TEMPER ETHOS WITH PATHOS

– your policies and platform may be 100 percent plausible, but people remember most the manner in which you deliver them. Ethos defines your character, code and philosophy. It is good that you let the people know your principles from the beginning. However, people relate to you first at the emotional level (pathos) before they do so at the intellectual level. If you can persuade people through strong emotive content, you will have won them intellectually. Most people consider overtly intellectual politicians as academic, flat and uninteresting. Although the electorate or voters may know you as a great political asset, they first want to see you happy, sad, attached to them and affected by what affects them. In short, *people do not care about how much you know until they know how much you care for them.*

RULE #47. SAY THE NAMES

– you cannot illustrate your views through nameless phantoms. You should showcase real people with real names and existence as your props for illustration. For example, if you want to show people how the last government's policies did not work, bring real persons who suffered poverty as a result. Name them and if possible, bring them out – who they are, where they are and what they said about the last government's policies. In doing so, however, consider the law regarding privacy and unsolicited disclosure.

RULE #48. TAKE CREDIT IF AND WHENEVER POSSIBLE

– in politics, you are looking for ways to take credit for victories, successes and good developments. You must work hard to make strong connections to you for good things. People love politicians who seem to be delivering and they feel better if they hear from their own politician. Sometimes, if no-one is taking credit for some good happenstance, as politicians find a connection to you and claim the credit unless there is clearly another politician who could take the credit. Even if another has taken credit, find an angle that can enable you to associate the victory to you or your party.

RULE #49. DON'T ARGUE WITH A CADER OR VOTER

– in politics, a cader or voter is always right. Even if you are insulted because of your politics or policies, always defer to the person. Do not try to reiterate; just swallow your pride and move on. In fact, if possible, tell the cader or voter that they are right and that you will ask for their votes so that you could align your platform to their view. Do not try to humiliate a cader or voter in public however strong they may have come at you. The same person who may hate you today, may love you tomorrow. That's the nature of politics.

RULE #50. DO NO HARM

– however frustrated, tired or disappointed you may be or feel, do no harm. Say nothing that you should be explaining later. Do nothing that should make you explain tomorrow. Avoid historically charged epithets. Disengage in name-calling, if you can prevent it. Don't attack children – even if they are the children of your opponents. Even if your caders are moving you to racially or tribally attacking your opponent, resist the temptation. History will pour scorn on your politics.

RULE #51. COAL MINE CONCEPT

- politics is like working in a coal mine wearing white clothes. No matter how careful you might be, you will end up being soiled by the contaminated political environment. The rule is to keep working and when all duty is finished you can change the soiled clothes and wear new apparel. The only ones who fail in politics are those who focus on the corrupt and overlook to do the people's bidding.

RULE #52. GOOD MEN MUST DO POLITICS

- a coward, politically speaking, is a man or woman who thinks that because their names will be made dirty by politics, therefore, bad men and women should rule. Politicians rely on the weakness of one in order, temporarily, to promote another. Past behavior and mistakes must be turned into assets to advance politically. And, in the interim, being a scandal can be detrimental unless, in the long run, one learns to accept the past and glory in the present. Even the worst scandal, politically, may be a catalyst to popular ascendancy if the politician learns to take it to the people and seek their understanding. When a person is exposed for things that they could not find courage to disclose, it is a question of liberty more than of lying or credibility. What matters in politics is the wellbeing of the general public and not the indiscretion of an individual.

RULE #53. COMPROMISE IS THE BACKBONE OF POLITICS

39

- if you can't compromise in politics, you can't win the race or complete the term.

ABOUT THE AUTHOR

Charles Mwewa (LLB, BA. Edu. + Engl., BA. Legal
Studies, Cert. Law, DIBM., LLM.) is a Dad, author, and
poet. Mwewa is the author of over 50 books and counting
in all genres – fiction (novels), non-fiction and poetry.
Mwewa, his wife, and their three girls, reside in the Capital
City of Ottawa, Canada

Websites:
charlesmwewa.com
acpress.ca

Facebook:
https://www.facebook.com/authorcharlesmwewa

Email:
info@acpress.ca

Amazon:
https://www.amazon.ca/dp/170346771X

INDEX

www.ingramcontent.com/pod-product-compliance
Lightning Source LLC
Chambersburg PA
CBHW051416250726
48655CB00003B/1081